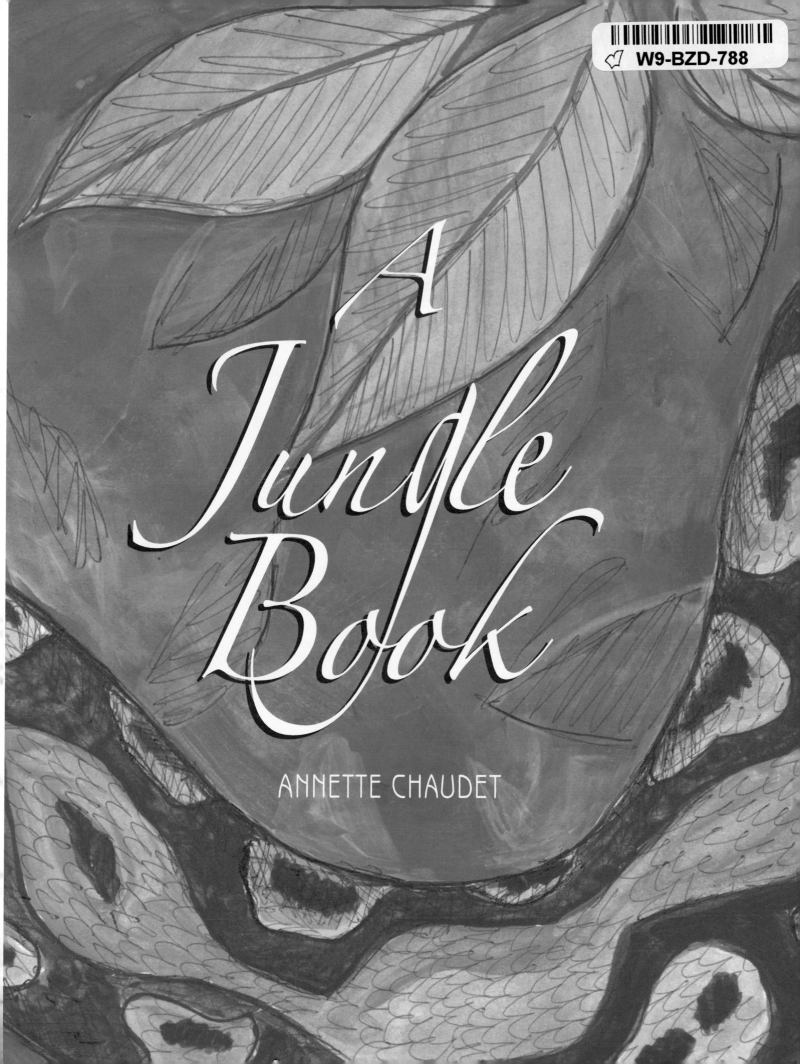

A Jungle Book

ANNETTE CHAUDET

Copyright 2008 Annette Chaudet

ISBN# 978-1-932636-41-3 Softcover

Library of Congress Control Number: 2007943690

Cover Design: Antelope Design
Illustrations: Annette Chaudet

Prairie Winkle

www.pronghornpress.org

Here you have a jungle book.
What jungle will it be?
For there are jungles everywhere
by the mountains and the seas.
There are jungles off in Thailand,
Jungles Indonesian,
Jungles South American,
Jungles Polynesian.
But THIS jungle's in Africa
where all these creatures roam,
so turn the pages, read the words
and see who calls it home!

Zebra

How dare you suggest
that one such as I
looks just like my friends
to the left or the right?
Can't you see we're all different,
unique as can be?
Not a one of these hundreds
is exactly like me.

It's true we all dress
in the same basic style
But it's simply high fashion
for those in the wild.

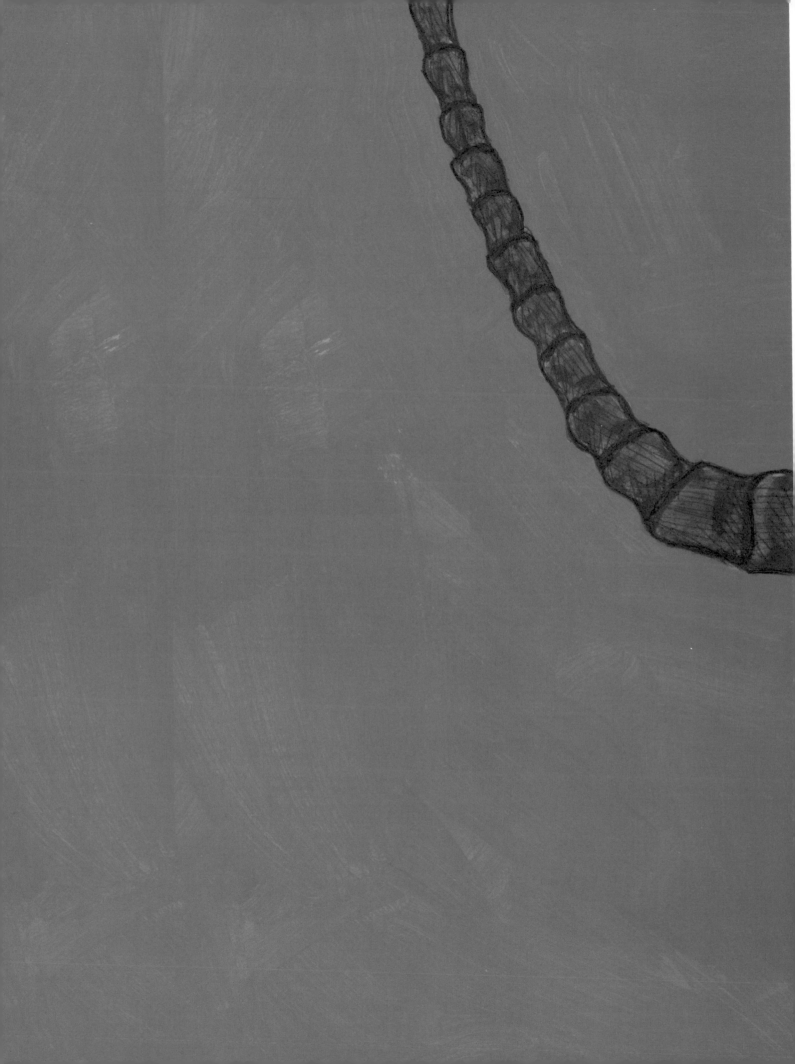

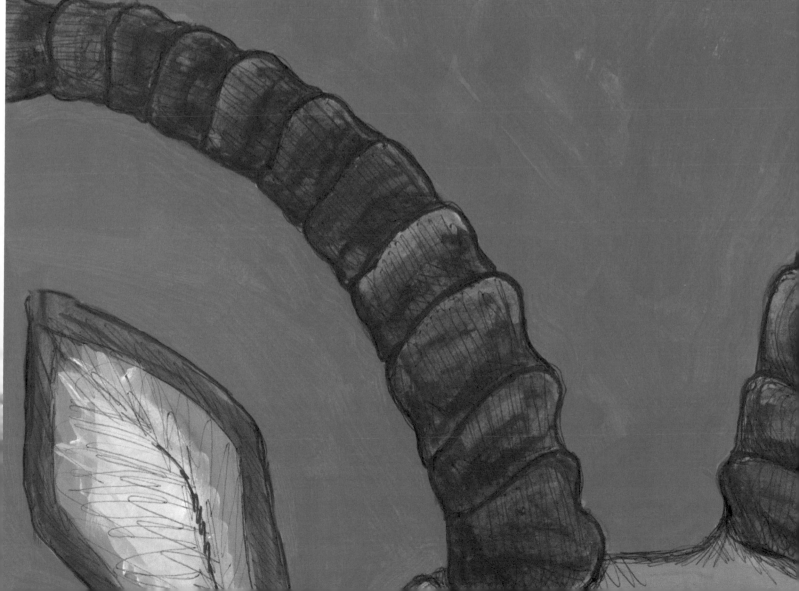

Impala

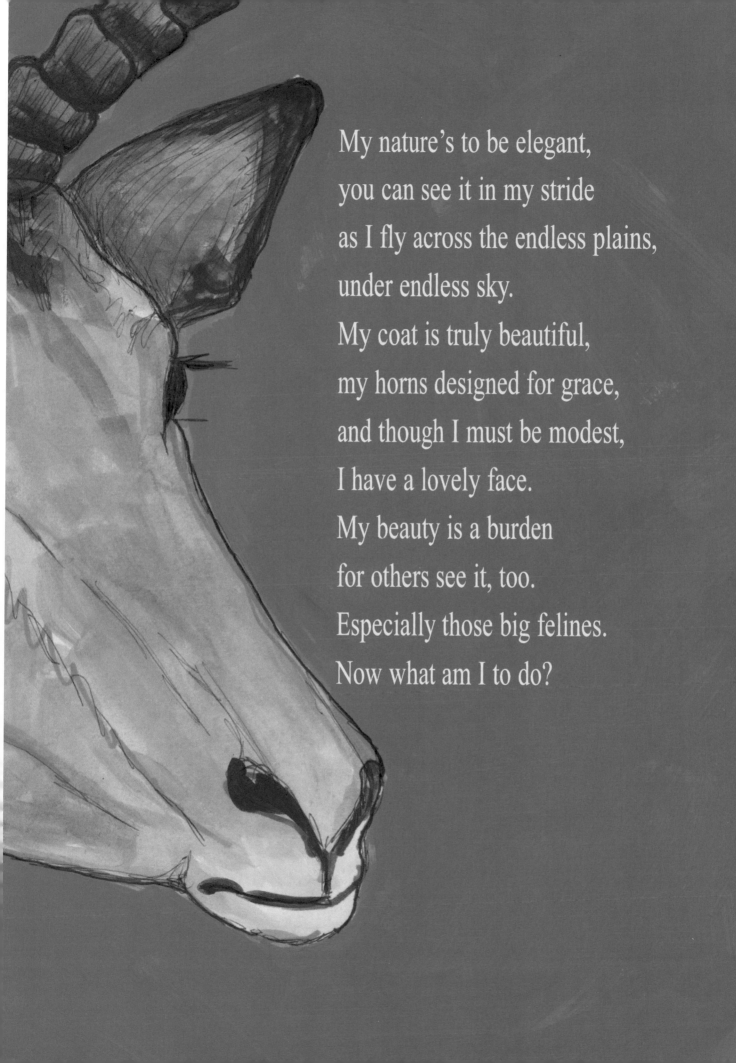

My nature's to be elegant,
you can see it in my stride
as I fly across the endless plains,
under endless sky.

My coat is truly beautiful,
my horns designed for grace,
and though I must be modest,
I have a lovely face.

My beauty is a burden
for others see it, too.
Especially those big felines.
Now what am I to do?

Giraffe

The view up here
is fine and clear,
but I see you stare
from way down there.
At your poor height
how do you know
just where it is
you want to go?

You dare call me clumsy?!
You say that I'm fat?!
Well, listen here, you,
I'll say this about that!
I'm graceful in water,
in rivers and streams.
I glide like a dancer
adrift in a dream.
I move very slowly,
with considerable grace,
So say nothing more.
Wipe that smile off your face!

I wonder if you g-know
I'm also a G-nu.
Though oddly put together,
I'm a perfect creature, too.
I am designed quite sensibly
for my G-nuly life
and I live it very happily
with my G-nuly wife.
We migrate 'cross the grasslands
in huge G-nuly herds
waiting for the springtime rain,
accompanied by the birds.

Elephant

It's good to be big.
It's grand to be tall.
Yet sometimes I wonder
what it's like to be small.

If you're little –
as far as I can see –
some might push you
who'd never push me.
So though I am big
and though I am slow
I always go just
where I want to go.

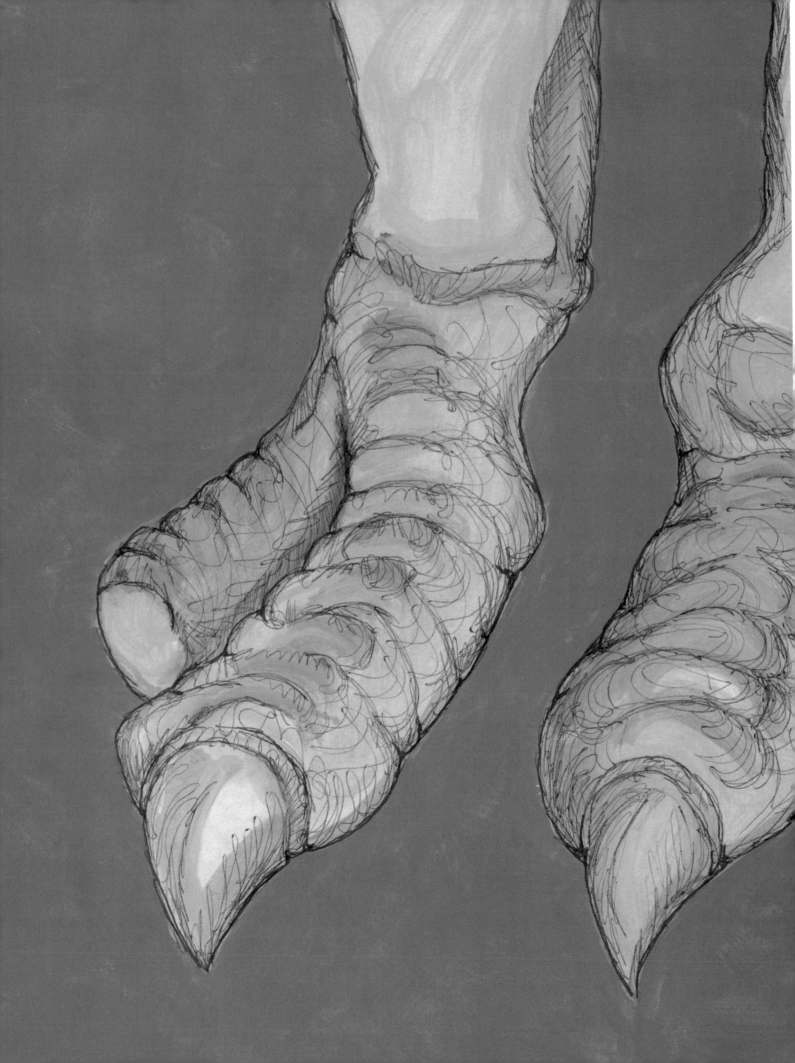

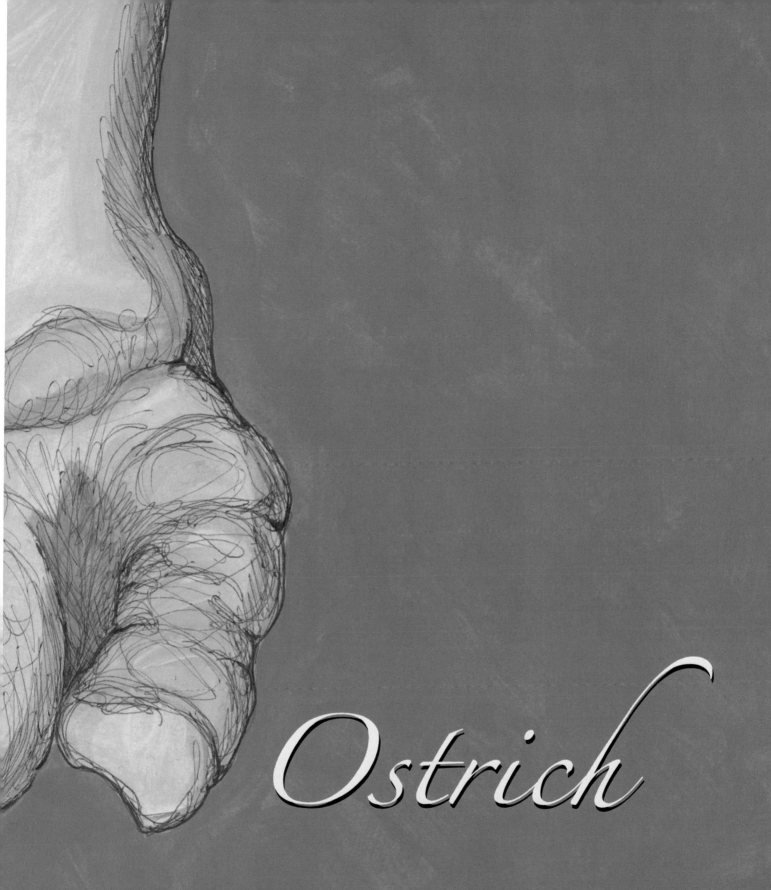

Ostrich

How dare you suggest

that my form's less than grand?

I'm one perfect part

of the Earth's perfect plan.

No, my wings aren't for flying

and my neck is quite long,

but I'm a great runner,

so what could be wrong?

I can run with the swiftest.

I've run races. Plenty!

And my egg makes a fine

morning breakfast for twenty.

Gorilla

We're smarter than you think—
my cousin KoKo's learned to sign.
But I wouldn't want to leave here.
This lifestyle suits me fine.
I spend my days in eating
and in napping 'neath the trees
and sometimes there are visitors
from far across the seas.
I hope that people understand
we creatures are all One,
and we must care for everyone
beneath the shining sun.

Vulture

High up in the sky,
wings spread, I glide
circling on thermals
for a lesiurely ride.
But I keep my eyes open
and watch for a meal.
Though others prepare it,
I'm happy to steal.
I don't do the killing
and so have no stress.
When it's all over,
I clean up the mess.

Crocodile

When I float like a log
at the edge of the river
if the animals see me,
they all start to shiver.
There's fear in their hearts
when they come here to drink.
The poor little dears,
they'd better not blink...

for I'm always watching.
I can hear their hearts beat.
I'm really not bad—
I just want to eat.

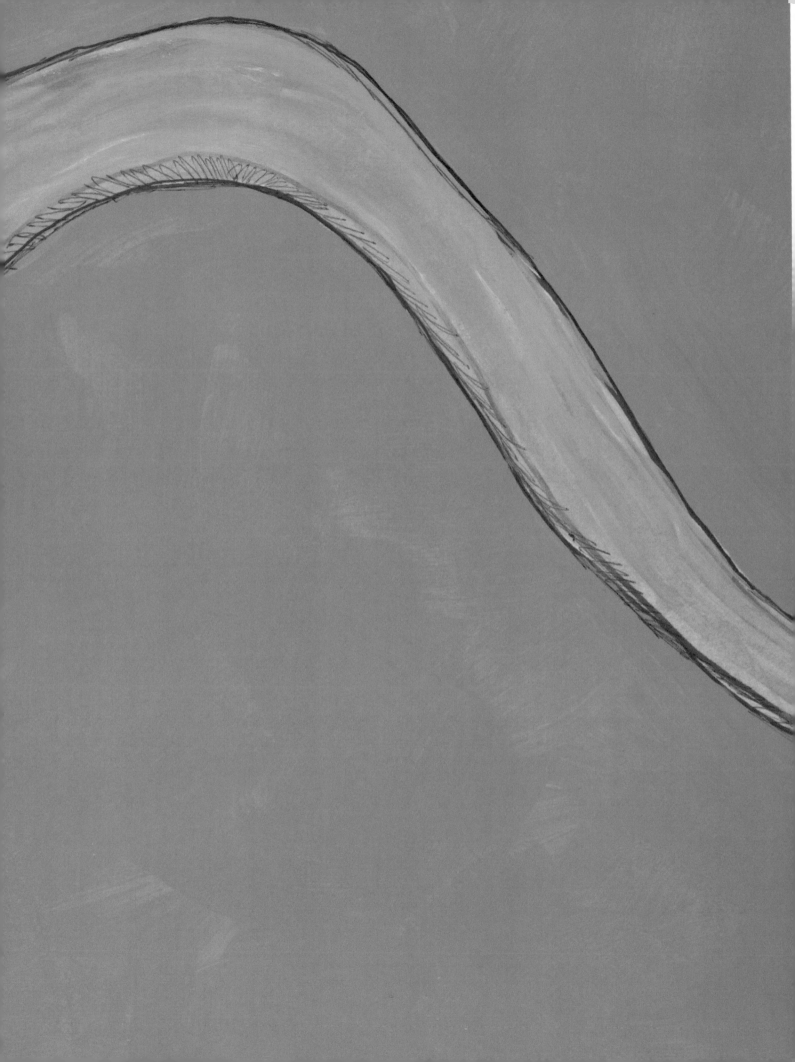

Lion

I've waited here
a night and a day.
I'm tired of sleeping.
I don't want to play.
My mate went out
for Dik Dik Delight.
I'm hungry.
I hope she comes back tonight.

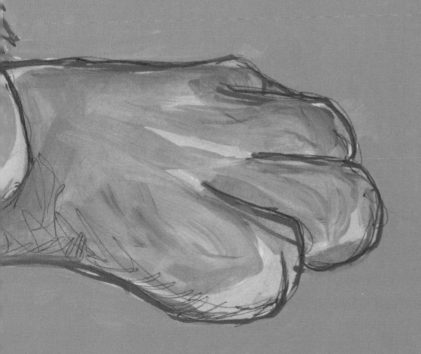

Rhinoceros

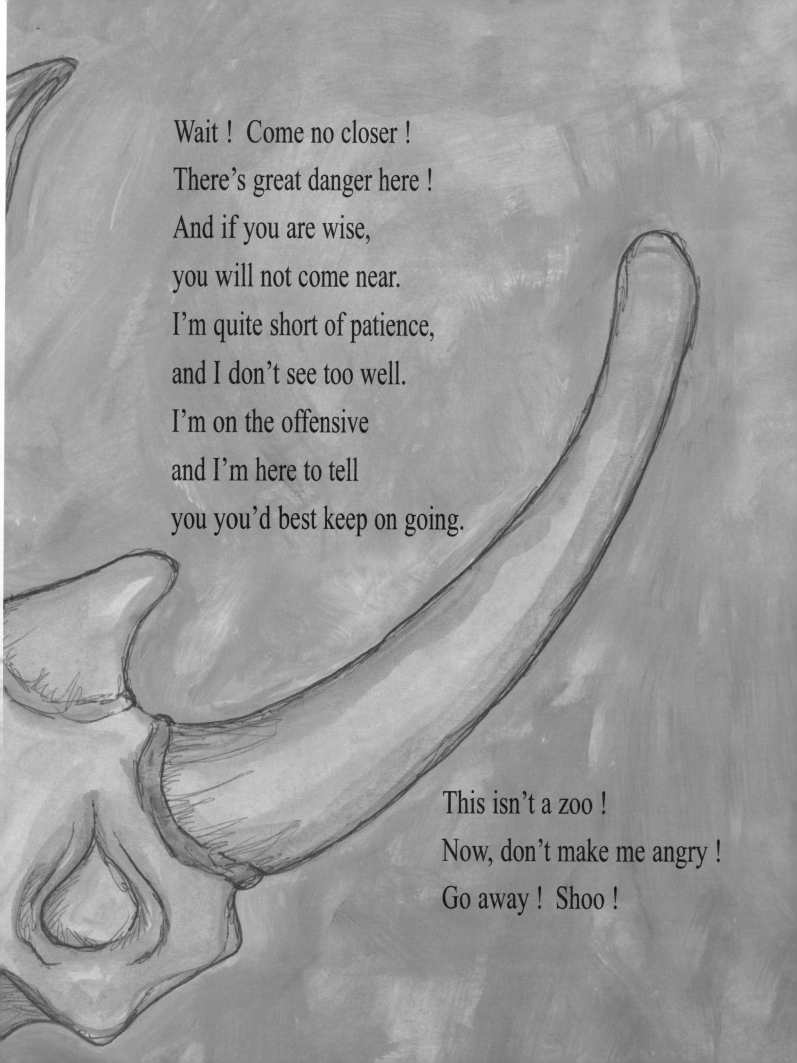

Wait ! Come no closer !
There's great danger here !
And if you are wise,
you will not come near.
I'm quite short of patience,
and I don't see too well.
I'm on the offensive
and I'm here to tell
you you'd best keep on going.

This isn't a zoo !
Now, don't make me angry !
Go away ! Shoo !

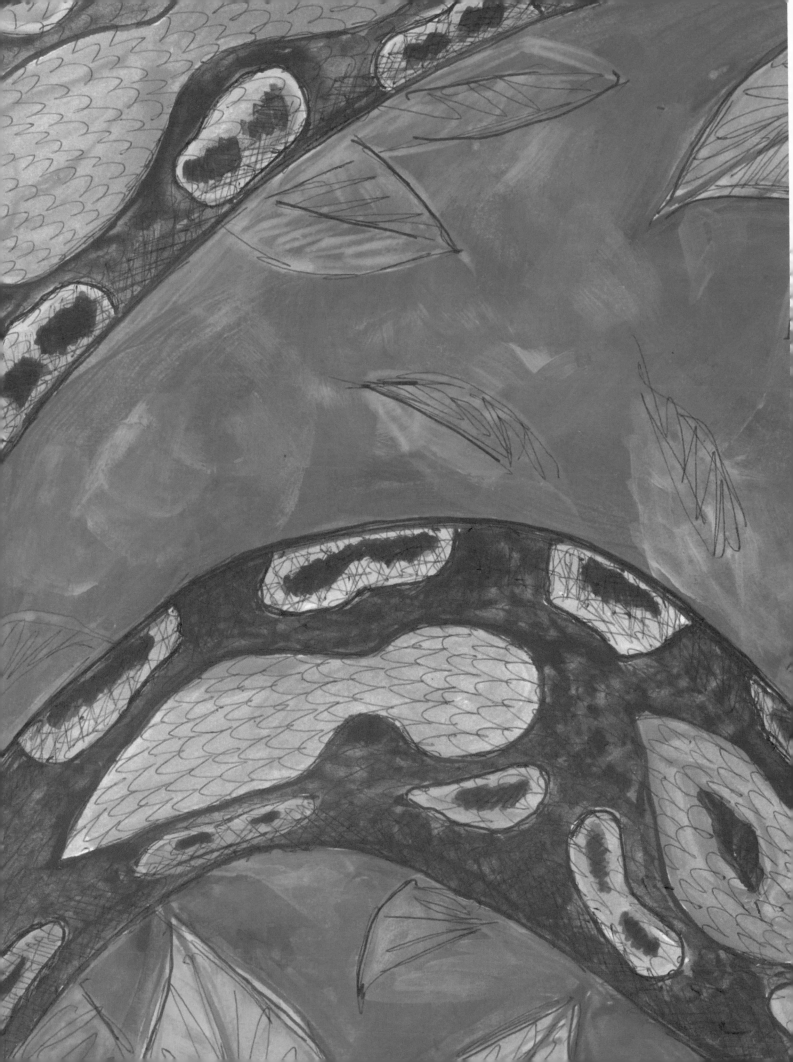

I've earned my name, believe me.
It's perfect, for I'm Royal.
And mind you I am quite a snake,
not just any coil.
I have a lovely pattern
and me it truly suits
but means—unfortunately—
that I may end up as boots.
Just because I am admired,
my kind is nearly gone.
So if you come upon me,
just say "Hi!" and move along.

Hyena

If you laugh at me, why,
then I'll laugh at you!
(though it may seem a rude
impolite thing to do.)
But that's how I got
my name, don't you see?
And laughing is just
part of me being me.
So when crossing these grasslands,
mile after mile,
if you hear me laughing,
please, won't you smile?

Cheetah